IRON MAN FAMILY OUTING

poems about transition into
a more conscious manhood

RICK BELDEN

art by john dolley

Rick Belden
www.rickbelden.com

ISBN 0-911051-56-2
Library of Congress Number 90-062745

several of the poems in this book have appeared
previously in the following publications:

Art-Core
The Austin Chronicle
Austin Men's Center Newsletter
Axis
Bull Horn
Pudding

Iron Man is a trademark of the
Marvel Entertainment Group, Inc.

thanks reviewers friends + supporters

chris belden
peter connery
barbara connery
don fehd
ted gowin
mike meacham

scott moehnke
dan morris
gina morris
amanda rose
steve sanderson
nell veeder

tuesday + wednesday men's support groups
eight guys who are not robert bly
roosti mabel + harriet.

thanks caregivers guides + healers

norma bell
russell bramlett
angela bumstead
caitlin burich
dan jones

john lee
jeannette miether
alice pryor
rick rose
carla wilson.

thanks marvel comics
for bringing iron man to
a small boy in need of a hero.

thanks david jewell
for insight encouragement + editorial support.

thanks john dolley
for bringing my visions to life so beautifully.

thanks susan bright + plain view press
for accepting + supporting this project + helping
with the nuts + bolts.

thanks great spirit
for crazy dreams + the opportunity
to do this in my own way.

this book is dedicated to iron men everywhere
and to women + children who love them.

contents

part one: life behind this mask   1

    little iron man   3
    god at eleven   4
    love leaves hole   5
    dad I got   6
    penguins   9
    smarts   10
    telegram   12
    I want   13
    ibm   14

part two: hungry wounds   17

    black noise   19
    half-life   20
    pleasureland   22
    hooked   25
    safe sexx confession   26
    red monk   28
    one more time   29
    another fact of life   30

part three: dance of the unloved child   31

    alone with her   33
    good   34
    mother junkie   35
    winter on the way   36
    spike jam   37
    fused at the wound   39
    romance death rattle   40
    doorway   42
    yo-yo   43
    ice house   44

part four: iron man dreams   45

real father   47
curiosity shop   48
gift   50
judge   52
crazy armor   53
self-defense   54
puffy iron mama   55
frustration sequence   56
another face   57
role model   58
athena   59

part five: shadowland   61

fear zone   63
alone again   64
lunatic son   65
fever wheels   66
senseless   68
x-ray barbeque   69
harpies   70
red meat head games   72
disconnected   74

part six: the unclaimed soul   75

water long gone   77
elephant dream   78
charley horse   80
plastic bones   81
plow my heart   82
hoofbeats   84
close to it   85
bridge to gate   86
touch the water   87
pearls   88
grief   89
decision time again   90

part seven: hints of daylight 91

starfall 93
difficult 94
brown-eyed boy 95
wounded man detection device 96
body memory 98
acceptance 99
learning to breathe 100
release 101
easter 102
autonomy 104
x-it wound 105
listen . . . 106

introduction

This is the story of my recent encounter with a childhood friend. Iron Man is a comic book super hero who wears a protective suit of armor with an electronically powered chest plate that keeps his damaged heart beating. The armor enhances his physical strength, allows him to fly, provides several powerful weapons, and protects him from severe blows and explosions such as the one that originally injured his heart. The armor is topped off by a menacing-looking helmet and face mask, which hide Iron Man's expressions and his identity from others. He's safe inside the armor, but almost totally isolated. No one can hurt him, but no one can touch him either. He does a lot of lying and covering up to keep those around him from knowing who's inside. He's sure that if the armor is removed, his wounded heart will stop and he'll die.

Iron Man was a boyhood passion of mine. Like many men I know, I grew up with an angry, abusive, unavailable father who was always working, even at home. He had no time or patience for me. I couldn't seem to please him, no matter what I did or how I did it. The effect of his behavior on the family was very destructive. My mom tried to hold it all together, but that caused other problems. No mother could have made up for the father I needed and didn't have. I grew up vowing to leave home as soon as I could, and swearing I would never be like him. I couldn't leave as a child, so I used my imagination to escape through fantasy. I pretended I was a cowboy, a soldier, a super hero. Of all the fictional heroes I tried to emulate, I identified most strongly with Iron Man. As a boy, I believed that if I could be Iron Man, I'd have it made.

I thought I'd said goodbye to Iron Man when I entered adolescence, but I found out last spring that I hadn't really finished with him yet. I began to have Iron Man dreams. I felt driven to find and collect the old Iron Man comic books I recalled from my youth. I made Iron Man collages and bought plastic Iron Man figures to play with. I felt a little crazy, but I decided to let my dreams and the little boy inside lead me through this, whatever it was. In the process, I reclaimed my lost creative energy, learned a lot about who I am, and found I was much more like my dad than I'd realized. I became aware of some of the reasons why I still needed to be Iron Man, even as an adult, and accepted Iron Man as a significant figure in the unique personal mythology I'd constructed for myself as a child. As I learned from Iron Man, my need for him diminished.

While I was working with the Iron Man metaphor, I kept a journal of dreams, thoughts, memories, and feelings. I also participated in a poetry workshop led by David Jewell at Austin Men's Center. My journaling and poetry workshop experiences inspired me to write a number of poems that explore issues and express feelings related both directly and indirectly to my inner life as Iron Man. These poems address my family and childhood experience, relationship issues, women, sex, work, dreams, and spirituality.

I've experienced a great deal of anxiety about how others, especially women, will perceive me through some of my writing. In order to develop a more positive view of my sexuality as a man, I have to work through a deep backlog of conflicting issues and mixed feelings around relationships, women, sex, and love. I've attempted to express that state of tension between new insights and old patterns as openly and directly as I could. I've actively chosen not to censor myself or apologize in advance for what I've written. I need to reveal myself as fully as possible and take the risk of being rejected for what I've tried to hide for so long. I hope I can do this without harming or alienating others. I need to share all my feelings in order to change, heal old wounds, and grow into a complete person.

My hope is that these poems show a man in conscious transition to becoming a better man and a better human being. It's an honest story of pain, awareness, struggle, and release, the story of an ongoing process of reunion and reconciliation with the child, the man, the animal, and the family inside my Iron Man armor. It works for me, and I sincerely hope that in your own way, it also works for you.

Rick Belden

part one

life behind this mask

little iron man

angry eyes burn behind cold metal mask
muscles tensed for fight in flight
repulsor rays   boot jets   armor
he is iron man.

all-powerful controller   master of his fate
vengeful righteous realist   almighty godlike hero
protector   judge   destroyer   martyr
invincible impervious inhuman.

mechanical masculinity   lover of the machine
better safe than sorry   greedy me-first hoarder
      dark doomy death dealer
      self-satisfying soul stealer
      childhood's chosen champion.

his armor
      once glistening   once wonderful
now binds and holds in place
      battle-scarred   time-tarnished   too small
      pitted   scorched   outdated   in the way
barrier to growth and love and life.

I tried to forget him
      but he came to me in dreams
I tried to kill him
      but he was stronger than I am
I tried to banish him
      but he wouldn't leave me
so I pulled off his grim metal mask.

a child's face   my face   revealed at last
frustrated   frightened   familiar   hopeful
      little boy with wounded heart
scared of the body he can't control
afraid to come outside   it hurts to be with people
a quarter century in an armor shell
      waiting for mommy and daddy to make it right.

god at eleven

god is an overdue library book
        an empty sardine can
        an angry santa claus.

god is a school bus full of strangers
        a sixty on the test
        a dad who's always pissed
        a mom with scar tissue.

god is a prison guard with rheumatic fever
        a flying squirrel in a cage
        a deformed colt in a field
        a member of the john birch society.

god still lives with his parents
he fights with his brother over pigs
        drives a milk truck on saturday to make ends meet
        makes me wear an athletic supporter
        watches *hee-haw* and listens to country music
            on the radio.

god has a workshop in the basement
he picks the dump and smokes white owls
        takes his teeth out when he eats
        makes me cry in front of the whole class
        stands in our driveway and tells my dad
            he's no good.

god wants to punish me for something I didn't do.

love leaves hole

falling knee   angry bowel
dad hates me
mother nurse   sick bitch   full bladder
tense muscles   wet grass   violent tyrant.

grim mask   empty armor
greasy hair   hammer whiskers
family violence   failure   puke
maximum disaster.

football courage   lunch box sadness
exposed terror   broken leg
sidewalk tyrant controls god
sidewalk love leaves me exposed.

hammer chest plate   control fear
love leaves hole
sidewalk disaster   mother panics
iron man dad explodes.

dad I got

he works
  five six seven days a week
  one two three jobs a week
  rotating shifts
  8 to 4
  4 to 12
  12 to 8
he works in a factory hates his job takes it out on us.

he chokes me when I want to see my friends
he leaves me behind
  I try to catch him I break my leg
he yells at me for hands in pockets
  humiliates me constantly in front of
    friends family neighbors strangers
he's angry + distant he scares me
he grabs my arm at the store + pulls me
  away from the girl I like
he tries to beat me down he
  tells me I'm flawed + worthless
  every chance he gets.

he yells at me when we go fishing
he yells at me when we go to church
he yells at me when we play ball
he yells at me when we're on vacation
he yells at me when I try to help him
  build the houses + fix the cars.

he tells me I throw like a girl
he tells me I'm not good enough
he tells me I'm no good
he tells me I'll never do it
he tells me I'll never amount to anything
he tells me I missed
  a spot here + a spot here + a spot here.

he works hard to pay the bills
he fights with his mother father brother sister
he treats my mom like property
        her family her friends like enemies
he builds a house for us to live in
he fights with the neighbors till we have to move
he builds another house
he gets mad at all the red lights
he thinks the world's against him.

he tells me not to laugh
he tells me not to cry
he has a flyswatter behind the sun visor to
        keep us in line while he's driving
he has no idea who I am
        shows no interest in finding out.

he scrapes my cheeks with sandpaper whiskers
        won't show me how to shave
        won't help me pick out my first car
        won't help me with college he buys
                another snowmobile instead
he tells me he doesn't care what happens to me
        if I go to texas.

he complains a lot when I ask for help then
        does it all himself
he burps a lot
he yells at me at the dinner table
        in restaurants
        until I get sick
he takes us to church because mom makes him do it
he loans me money for car insurance once
he uses anything he does for me
        against me later on.

he works at night sleeps during the day
        tells us to shut up when
        we're playing in the back yard

he can build anything
he can fix anything
he does the best he can
he hurts me.

he doesn't trust me
he spies on me
he kicks my ass across the yard in front of my friends
        because I'm late
he threatens to cut off my hair + mustache
        while I sleep
he slaps the soles of my feet to
        wake me up in the morning.

he goes to night school to learn a trade
he says everybody else is wrong
he acts like he doesn't want me
he acts like I'm in the way
he acts like I don't matter
he acts like he doesn't like me.

        I love him
        I need him
        I hate him
        I miss him.

this is the dad I got.

penguins

when I was 7 or 8
        I made these penguins out of paper-mache
actually as usual on this type of project
        seems like my dad did a lot of the work
we made two of them one big one little
        emperor and dwarf I think
they had wire hanger skeletons
        inside paper-mache bodies
I painted them and they looked real cool.

they were for a school project so
        they hung out at school for a while
        then I brought them home and
        gave them to my mom
she put them in her bedroom closet
        for safekeeping.

every so often I'd sneak in and look at them
        or ask mom to let me see them
        until one day they were gone!
I asked my mom where the penguins were and
        she said they got moldy
        so she threw 'em out
I never saw them again
        don't even have a picture
        except the blurry one in my head
I sure wish she had let me say goodbye to them
        or taken a picture of them
        or something
but they're gone for good and it really hurts.

I'm 31 goin' on 32 and
I still can't believe my mom did that.

smarts

I still need to be the smartest kid in the class.

at school I was finally able to establish
some sense of self-worth
        at home I felt lost
dad was impossible to please + mom
            who knows
I'm still working on that one
but I could kick some ass in the classroom
not just do well
but be the fucking STAR!
        approval from adults who mattered
        respect from other kids
I could INTIMIDATE the little bastards
keep them from getting too close
they might kick my butt on the playground
        or in gym class
but the rest of the day
THEIR ASSES WERE MINE
        everybody knew it
if another smart kid was around
(a boy -- girls didn't really count anyway)
        I resented the hell out of him
I wanted to destroy him any way I could
        academically or physically
(I knew that in a fistfight between wimps I would prevail).

I've carried this attitude into everything I've ever
        cared about since then.

in a relationship
with someone I consider a peer
I've got to be
        the more advanced
        the smarter one
        all the time.

I've got to have
        answers   more answers
        better answers   the right answers
        all the time
or I feel inadequate + resentful.

I've got to be
        the STAR!   the leader
        the big brother   the teacher's favorite
I've got to do
        the most creative advanced work
        in the most creative advanced group
all the time or I'm shit.

if I feel that someone else is doing better than I am
        I hate him + I want him to fail somehow
        so I can feel ok about who I am.

there's only one chance
there's only room for one star pupil
everyone else is worthless
        except for providing the star pupil
        with other people to be better than.

there's only room for one star pupil + I'm it
        or I'm nothing.

telegram

high school drag   boring prison
lovely whore   easy bitch
seat belt sex   wild animal   passion sadness.

wet bed   plastic shame   hopeless cover-up
out of shape   alone sad lonely.

math essential   writing impractical
work sucks   dope essential
don't know sadness   don't know love   no time
workworkworkworkwork broke me
dope expensive sex fix drunk diseased
my life sucks
work lies   sex lies   high school lies.

stop.

I want

I want my dad to give a damn
I want my mom to leave me alone
I want to be strong and lean again
        to do work I really like
        to stop hurting so much
I want people to like me
I want to stop being afraid of my body
I want sunshine + trees + fresh air
        good food + healthy sex
        a relationship that works
        a family that's not fucked-up
I want to be happy
I want to be loved
I want to stop feeling like god's sneakin' up on me.

ibm

mighty white
uptight
fight or flight
you're wrong we're right
bite in the soul.

a pile of money big enough to talk the
little tramp out of the grave into
modern times on the corporate assembly line
pitching pc's between first downs.

monkey work for everybody!
no job too big no mind too small.

slack jaw slack eyes slack face
superslack mondoslack
lamp-smashing drunken rage
apocalypse now
time off later
stuff it in the bank
stuff it in the gut
time for lunch.

think money drink money
spend money eat money live money
get fat get drunk get numb get dumb
get old get dead get out.

us versus them
we're cool   they're not
we're smart   they're not
we're people   they're not.

no windows no sun no plants no sky no trees no animals
pale yellow walls
beige carpet
fluorescent lights

stagnant air
temperature extremes
drop ceiling
formaldehyde maze
big styro egg carton
humpty dumpty eunuchs.

endless meetings where
     nothing happens but tick tick tick
wander around staring at my watch for
     3 months
     6 months
     9 months
chained to a pipe dream while
blank walls + blank stares + blank checks
gnaw + claw at
     my liver my stomach my colon my prostate
     my back my legs my heart my soul my will.

afraid to leave
afraid to live
afraid to love.

afraid to rock the titanic
     as if I could tip it over anyway
     which I'd love to if I had the chance.

afraid this prefab hell on earth won't
     take me back again if I
     leave ahead of schedule
     this time around.

afraid I'll knock over all the other dominos if I
     open the door + walk out right now.

afraid I'll hammer myself into a
     black hole if I don't.

I hate your self-satisfied blank bloodless lying smirking
        narrow-minded animal-paving sleep-inducing
        paranoid mediocre spy versus spy
better safe than sorry death insurance.

I hate your keep quiet pay the undertaker
        interchangeable white male rubber stamp
        compartmentalized departmentalized
        equal opportunity security begins with you
be just like me party line.

you can keep your easy money death rattle + your
        ivory tower missile silos + your
        faceless nameless corporate cult + your
big blue zombie massage parlor.

save them for the next sell out shoot up
        get rich quick retire in 10 years
        gold-digging grave-digging
laptop billy the kid
there's one born every minute you know
everyone's got good reasons to be seduced but
        not me
        not by you
        not this time
        not this tomb.

I've had enough
I'm out
it's over
I'm gone
I won't be back.

so when does reality set in?   *this is it.*

and what will I do now?   *something else.*

part two

———————■———————

hungry wounds

black noise

last night
after a very unsatisfying men's group
I went to the granite cafe + had pizza + cheesecake
tried to dump my guts on my girl friend
but she didn't want 'em
so I went to the yellow rose + on the way there
it really started to hit me
that I'm not gonna get that dad I wanted
but I sure as hell didn't wanna deal with THAT
at midnight on koenig lane
so I dropped 60 $$$ on 5 couch dances
a beer + a shot of tequila
then came home drank 3 dixie beers + 2
or was it 3 more tequila shots
wandered up + down the street outside the house
raving to myself about how fucked
all this self-awareness crap is + I swore off
poetry + men's groups + twelve steps + flying boys
+ I swore off the wild man dogma machine I mean
how hard can all this be anyway just use common sense
who needs to make a big goddam project out of it + I
listened to gimme shelter/satisfaction/harvest/grave concern
long dark road/have mercy on the criminal
until I woke up this morning in a blast of white light
+ shit + puked + puked + puked + when
I was puking this black stuff came
out of my stomach + this black noise
came out of my guts + now it's
3 o'clock + I've slept the whole
damn day.

half-life

I try and try but I can't always get it
        what does he want from me anyway?
I'll drive anywhere pay anything
        do anything to get that guy
        off my back for an hour or two.

what's the half-life of a lousy childhood?
stranglehold tentacles
        come out of a house where
        nobody I know lives anymore
body and soul clench like a fist
        when that hairy hand tries to pull me down
I need lights   I need noise
        I need naked female flesh all around
else I implode.

how do I give up what I don't understand?
this home isn't broken it's blown to hell.

now *here's* a place where I can be unhappy in peace
totally safe and unbelievable
a crime against everything I was brought up to be
a slap in the face to that guy who thinks
        he knows how it's supposed to be done
a tight connection to all those old friends
        I thought I'd left behind
whores just like me
who knows what they sell themselves for?

last chance for ro-mance
take care of these ladies and they'll take care of you
        why do I need this?

the weird thing is I don't even see
        most of these women anymore
                not even as objects.

20

can't buy a thrill?
sometimes I can sometimes I can't but
       I don't need a thrill
       I need a break.

pleasureland

scary peroxide blonde with huge breasts prances around
    with a leather belt attached to her neck like a leash
smiles as she invites men to whip her bare ass.

klansman in white hood + robes fucks
    laughing black girl in cheap motel room
oriental woman bound + gagged chained to a wheel
    spins around   little whips flick at her naked skin
skinny little effeminate man   he looks sick   suspended by
    his arms from the ceiling
    red plastic ball taped into his mouth
    angry woman what a nazi
    hits him   tells him he's shit
later on two big guys rape him.

video tapes + magazines
organized by special interest
    bisexuals lesbians she-males frat boys
    big tits butt fucks blow jobs fat women
    bondage rape + torture
it all looks like pain to me tonight.

every face in every picture says
    love me i'm bad i hate myself
    hurt me let me hurt you
    i need to feel something i'm helpless take me
    i need to feel loved
    if we hurt each other we will feel loved.

gay straight fat black white
men + women   bound + gagged
wounded + desperate
unloved children in grown-up bodies.

degradation   exploitation
domination   subjugation
soul abuse   arousal.

most of all the bondage
too much!
intense photos on video boxes
  women strapped to boards
  bound in leather + ropes
  contorted + tied into pretzel shapes
  gagged with large red rubber balls in their mouths
    fear in their eyes
    helpless . . .
  hurt me i like it i like to be hurt
  it's ok to hurt other people
  they want you to hurt them
  they get off on it.

angry aroused curious outraged confused
  I want to see this
  no I don't
  just a little
  I've seen enough
  just once
  no!

this time I can't do it
I can't watch this or bring it into my home
  without violating that little boy inside
hasn't there been enough of that already?

a struggle
  I'm drawn like a moth to a headlight
  like a cat into a
    warm engine spinning radiator fan
    on a cold winter morning.

this stuff appeals to everything that's
  wounded + dysfunctional in me
prepackaged soul abuse
  choose life!

does any of this turn you on

I used to think those people on the corner were nuts
	pornography is child abuse
don't take my word for it
see for yourself.

women + children don't count for much in this culture
	nobody does
life's cheap
	I'm not kidding check it out.

all this + still I have a need
I go home disgusted   go to bed
	jack off thinking about an old girl friend
	somebody else's wife
not very satisfying at all.

I used to feel guilty + relieved after masturbation
now I just wish I'd done something else instead.

hooked

naked young women with fishing poles
      dance inside my eyes
their hooks waiting restlessly within my chest
      memories of hot female sway
I tug at their lines
      they reel me in.

safe sexx confession

she sits down beside me
she tells me
      I'm nasty can you handle it
she slides out of her leather skirt
she pins me into a chair in the corner
she looks me right in the eyes
she rubs her body all over mine
she says
      you like head don't you
she touches my hardness through my pants + says
      impressive
she tells me about her dreams
she wears a black push-up bra
she asks me
      do you like to tit fuck
she grabs my cock through my pants over + over
she says
      you like to fuck from behind doggie style
      in front of a mirror don't you
she turns me on
she scares the hell out of me
she gives me the teeth chatter chills
she gives me the first date shits
she makes me wait forever
she says
      imagine you're inside me right now
she takes my hands off her breasts when I
      try to touch them
she tells me she knows it's a power trip
she says
      I can tell you're a great lover 'cause
      you have a very sensitive cock
she lets me run my hands up her
      thighs + around her cheeks
she has a catholic father + a baptist mother
she laughs about her sins
she jokes about confession

she tells me this is safe sex
she says
> *slide down in the chair so I can*
> *rub against your crotch*
she knows a lot about me somehow
she tells me
> *you're too hot to stay in an unhappy relationship*
she puts her clothes back on
she says goodnight
she walks away
she gives me back
> something I thought was lost for good
> something I thought I didn't
>> deserve anymore anyway.

she leaves me
> hot hard swollen animal-buzzing
> electrified + alive again at last.

red monk

depth of feeling
intensity of feeling
explosion of feeling
absence of feeling.

the chocolate tiger waits for the red monk
        to finish his rounds + come clean
hides in the bushes + spies on him
        like a hungry god
        like an empty house
waiting to swallow him up.

one more time

I've got a belly fulla meat
I've got a belly fulla cheese
I've got 250 snappy replies
        for a phone call that's never gonna come
I haunt my body like an unemployed ghost
I drive to the post office on a holy crusade
I walk through the world encased in glass
I fight the system
I am the system
I drink down illusions on an empty stomach
        + vomit nervous shadows at twilight.

but a shot of hip-grinding light flash
        gives me reasons
        keeps me real
        saves me from the bloodless void
I touch a thigh   an elbow   a shoulder
I leap into her eyes
she smiles + licks her lips
fucked-up + lovely
        she kisses my cheek
I flicker to life for one brief moment
my heart turns the same old corner
        one more time.

jaded + vulnerable
my heart hits the same old wall
        one more time.

another fact of life

I've recently realized that
       among other things
       my father + I have
never discussed sex in any way
whatsoever.

dad I know you were pretty busy
       but I feel like you
left out something kind of important
here.

part three

dance of the unloved child

alone with her

dreaming again.

she and I are in my truck
       I'm driving through a storm
we've had another chance meeting
       this time she's agreed to come with me.

she's being careful about all this
       slow shy + tentative
I'm freaking out
       going much too fast for the conditions
              downhill on a slick road
              poor visibility + a steep drop-off on one side
       but I'm having a bad anxiety attack
       and I've got to find a safe place fast
before I lose my shit in front of her.

I pull into one of those gasstationconveniencestores
I go inside to pay for some gas
she stays in the truck
       I'll be right back.

there are two men my age inside the store
       cutting up
       shooting the breeze
       joking around
I feel safer in here.

I spend far too much time inside
       talking with the guys about nothing
       while she waits outside in the rain
because I'm too afraid to be alone with her.

good

see her
smell her belly
rub her thighs
bury my face in her pussy
see that look in her eyes
        when I slip between her legs
feel her tongue in my mouth
feel our bodies catch fire
        as she takes me in
lay with her
        inside her after we've come
feel + smell + hear her come
hear her moaning
        moaning for me
        reaching for me
all right already
        sucking + stroking + fucking
that wonderful body I've admired
        so many times.

I want this
this is healthy
this is good.

mother junkie

mother junkie has found a new fix
      lonely + desperate
      sick of trying
      tired of waiting
      this is the one.

no second thoughts
he takes her straight in
      straight into his veins
      straight into his bones
a double shot of morphine
      right between the eyes
the visions come
fairy tale poison
      she can save me.

no more pain
      he lives again
no more doubt
      he is strong again
no more fear
      he is free again.

for now.

winter on the way

mid-august
austin texas
one pm
ninety degrees.

on the sidewalk in front of our house
      kneeling to pet her cat
the palm of my hand touches him + I feel it:

    this isn't going to last.

spike jam

she jams me up
she shuts me down
she talks too much.

she ties me up in careful knots
       thins my experience
       dilutes my passion with
best intention mother smother
platitude chatter instant analysis
wall of words head trip charm
emotional detours.

she really tries   I know she does   so do I
I start to feel   I speak   she counters
she starts a sentence she doesn't finish
       I've seen this one before.

she goes away
       miles away
she goes inside
       deep inside
I'm there alone   I wait   I listen
       hostage to a conversation for
       seconds minutes hours days
       years decades lifetimes.

my heart + brain are pumping fast
it's ok   I'm patient
I know I can handle it
I wanna say
       FINISH THE GODDAM SENTENCE!!!
but I wait
she finally says some words
they don't make sense
they're muddled fuzzy
       wishy-washy watered down.

she waters me down
she talks me down
she talks me out of my fragile moment.

I jam up   shut down   shut up
I'm angry   I short circuit
I can't speak   I can't feel
I can't stand it
I go away.

fused at the wound

is it love or is it addiction
        why not both
she knows tears + I know anger
together we almost made a whole person for a while
fused at the wound.

but our little house of lies isn't big enough to hold us now
she won't stand up for herself + I can't stand up
        for both of us at the same time anymore
so we ride the broken lover's seesaw of staying + leaving
        one foot in + one foot out
we dance in the kitchen like unloved children + wait
        for fulfillment of old pain's expectations.

so anxious to leave   so anxious to be left
so anxious to be right   so anxious to be hurt
so anxious to be disappointed
so anxious to be alone again.

when this whole thing started
        I wanted us to be immersed in each other
        I wanted us to fix each other
        I thought that was what people were supposed to do
I don't want that anymore
I don't need that anymore
        but I still don't know
                how to love someone I don't want to fix.

romance death rattle

wild animal lays injured in the street
saturday night cars zoom past
     uncaring
     barely missing
breath comes in halting irregular painful spasms
struggle to live.

man stops
pokes the animal with a hammer handle + says
     it's dead it just don't know it yet
he's right
I can't save it
the best I can do tonight is watch it die.

sadness comes
     like a wave of bricks
     like a meteor shower
     like a razor blade blizzard.

sadness comes
     like a rib cage drill press
     like a sledgehammer shotgun
     like a breastbone ripsaw.

    work isn't   the answer
    food isn't   the answer
     sex isn't   the answer
  money isn't   the answer
    she isn't   the answer.

even the answer
     isn't the answer
         on a night like this
what was the question anyway?

she doesn't appreciate me   I don't appreciate her
        I'm not enough   she's not enough
                we're not enough
can't anybody tell me
        how to get one of these things to work?

we were wild once but now
        the ruts are too deep
we went to sleep together + woke up
        in separate beds in separate rooms in separate lives
how could I let this happen to me again?

if I leave now   I'm a quitter
If I don't leave   I'm a coward
if I leave now   I'm a coward
if I don't leave   I'm a liar.

I really need some sleep.

I thought we could leapfrog over our loneliness + sorrow
I tried to cut corners + now
        here I am
backed into one again.

all those conflicts we avoided
all those scary arguments we never had
all those times my soul said *wait*
        + my heart said *now please now.*

these are the things that pin me down + sit on my chest
        like a playground bully
                squeezing + stifling my affection for her
        until breath comes
in halting irregular painful spasms.

it's dead it just don't know it yet
        he's right
        I can't save this one either
the best I can do tonight is watch it die.

doorway

she sits on the couch in her room
      naked
      her back to me.

she trims her toenails while
      cool morning sun slips through the blinds
      and lays zebra stripes on her bare skin.

I stand in the doorway
      brushing my teeth
      taking her in
and wondering how much longer she'll be here with me.

yo-yo

my guts are unstable
I'm shitting fire
there's an animal rustling around in the dark
        outside my window
but I can't find it.

personality eclipse
dead flowers in the jar
what's for dinner
dirty laundry avalanche
I can't keep up with all this stuff.

we see that movie + here we go
        kids again
        she must be joking
I'm no father yet.

anyway
        she's leaving now
        she's staying now
        she's leaving now
pulling the string
up + down dizzy I go.

I never could understand how these things worked
        even as a kid
        no help from mom + dad.

might be time for me to let go.

ice house

cold weather is no innocent bystander
it stabs the heart like a gleaming ice pick
it peels back the skin like a fur trapper's knife
it runs through the bones like liquid hydrogen
     till steam comes out the nose
     till fingers crack + bleed
     till blood thickens + pools
till the house is empty at last.

part four

———————■———————

iron man dreams

real father (iron man dream #1)

I'm in one of the houses I lived in as a child.

I've discovered that the father I know
        the man who raised me
        isn't my real father after all
he's a substitute who adopted me
        after my real father was killed
my real father was iron man
        the *real* iron man.

the provider of this information is an old man
        a stranger.

I demand to know how iron man
        my father
                was killed
the old man asks me if I'm sure I want to know
I tell him I am
he plays a videotape of iron man's death
I watch it on a tv.

on the tape
        iron man flies toward
                a large fireball in the sky
it looks like the sun
suddenly
        as he comes close to it
                the fireball explodes.

the explosion is about to envelop + destroy him
the force of the blast will blow him apart.

I wake up screaming *NO!!!*

curiosity shop (iron man dream #2)

facing east I park the truck
is this the right direction?
inside the truck   some treasured things
       a box of rocks and childhood charms.

across the street   inside the shop
       a thousand things for second sale
big-bellied happy plastic goat
       in overalls and farmer's hat
a cardboard box   sedan inside
       IRON MAN FAMILY OUTING!
behind the wheel he's grim determined
       full armor   wife and kids.

the old man smiles
he's open   friendly
I feel distrustful   ill at ease
       my dad was iron man too he says
he knows too much to be a stranger.

old woman's voice is hard to hear
       immersed in static   broken   fading
she seeks the owner of a truck
she wants the box of charms and trinkets . . .

       your talismans are very bad
       it's not your fault   they came like this
       someone passed them on to you
       do not pass them to another
       let me clear the bad luck for you
       contact me   it's very urgent.

she gives her name and how to find her
I can't hear   there's too much noise.

young woman stands behind the counter
       tired of taking care of others

I ask her who the woman was
      the one who made the last announcement
she answers several times but I can never understand her
      please write it down
      I can't quite hear you
inside I feel embarrassed.

the writing on the card she hands me
      looks like nonsense   out of context
I fail to see how this will help me
the writing on the card is mine.

gift (iron man dream #3)

I'm in new york to visit my mom + dad
they're still living together
     in the house our family moved out of 20 years ago
they don't appear to have aged since that time.

my dad seems unhappy + remorseful about his life
     not the angry man I knew
he seems sad about his relationship with me + anxious
     to make some kind of connection between us.

he + I are standing in the
     big doorway of the garage he built
this is dad's territory
mom stays in the house.

he gives me a real old iron man comic book
     but first he goes through it
     tearing out stuff he says I'm not supposed to see
          stuff that has something to do with work
his deletions appear random to me
I can't see a pattern of anything sensitive
     in what he removes.

he describes in great detail the way iron man moves
     including the precise number of seconds it takes
          for iron man to respond to an attack
then dad asks me how long it takes
     for me to respond to an attack.

the iron man comic he gives me is a one time only
     special issue
this is the one I've been searching for
     the one where iron man's face mask changes
          from pointed + horned
          to rounded + smooth.

in this issue
        iron man reveals that he is actually a monk
when questioned
        he explains that the monk is the other side of
        his usual playboy/inventor/materialist identity.

in the dream
        I recognize this comic book as
                a very special gift from my dad
                        something important to him
                        something he's saved for a long time
it's a peace offering
        something we both value.

in the dream
        I feel touched yet saddened
our communication is still so indirect.

a comic book is no substitute
        for a warm hug + loving words
        between a father + a son.

judge (iron man dream #4)

I'm sitting in a town meeting
     in the roman catholic church I attended as a boy
there are lots of people but
     the church is far from being filled up.

one of my old high school teachers
     one of the few I liked
          stands at the lectern
he's the leader of this meeting.

I'm wearing my iron man costume
it's not real armor it's just a costume
     but it's very authentic-looking.

my old teacher's trying to pass himself off as
     some sort of community leader but
          I feel he is too soft too weak
               a hypocrite.

I'm armed with a set of
     potentially damaging questions
I plan to confront him with them publicly
     in this meeting
I believe my questions will
     prove his hypocrisy + weakness
     destroy his credibility as community leader
I'm acting
     not out of a feeling of malice but
     out of a sense of duty to the others
everyone must know the truth about this man.

I feel safe exposing him because
     I'm in my iron man costume.

crazy armor (iron man dream #5)

I'm in a bookstore
they've got a whole section of books about iron man
   I buy two of these iron man books.

I find a passage in one of them
   in which the author quotes a conversation
   between iron man and his best friend
his friend recites a long list of names
   others who have worn the armor
   prior to the current iron man
his friend remarks that
   no matter who wears the armor
   they always get that crazy look in their eye
   when they put it on
he says the only way a man
   can wear the armor successfully
   is to get a little crazy
he recalls his fondness for
   iron man's vulnerable period as an adolescent
     a young boy
   before he was fully armored.

I bring my iron man books home
   and tell my mom about them
she's concerned
these books have many drawings and describe
   the progression from one armor to the next
mom's worried that having this information
   will somehow interfere with my progress.

at this point she changes from my mom to my girl friend.

self-defense (iron man dream #6)

I'm in my office at home
I've accidentally left my journals out
a page from one of them
        is being projected onto the wall
        by some sort of device
my mom walks into the room.

I don't want her to see what's in my journals.

the page that's currently projected on the wall
        is ok for her to see but
this device is capable of advancing independently
        from one page to the next
and I'm not sure about what might be coming up.

she makes a remark to the effect that
        my writing is hard to read but
        there's a nice visual rhythm to it
her remark seems terribly superficial to me
she's not interested at all in
        what I'm saying
        only how it looks
I feel myself closing up in frustration.

when she's not looking
        I close the journal
leaving an image of the cover
        a picture of iron man
projected on the wall.

puffy iron mama (iron man dream #7)

I've been gone for a while.

when I come back into the family area
        my mom says to me
                very sarcastically
                welcome home   it's about time you got back
                        how was your break?

in this dream
        my mom is a giant oversized bloated balloonish
                puffy marshmallow iron man
        wearing an apron and holding a broom.

frustration sequence (iron man dream #8)

I'm cutting up an iron man comic book with some scissors
        just like I used to as a boy
I want to
        collect some pictures of iron man for my book
        arrange them in a meaningful sequence
but it's not going too well.

I can't get the sequence right
        I keep making mistakes
I'm cutting in the wrong places
        I don't have time for this
I don't understand why this is taking so long
        I thought I'd be done by now
this shouldn't be so hard for me
        I'm getting frustrated . . .
WHY DON'T I KNOW HOW TO DO IT?

in the comic book that I'm cutting up
        iron man is trying to escape from a prison
        but he keeps getting caught.

another face (iron man dream #9)

I'm looking at a picture of the new iron man
his armor's been redesigned
I don't like it.

the new armor has no face mask
his face is completely exposed!

the old iron man
        the one I knew
has been replaced by some younger guy.

the old iron man was dark angry + intense
        an injured soul fighting to survive
this new guy looks like some stereotypical
        california surfer dude
                blond-haired + blue-eyed
                muscled-up + bland-handsome
another pretty beach party boy.

I don't care for these changes at all
I don't get it
I can't relate
who are they trying to kid?

without his mask
        without his darkness
                iron man is just another face in the crowd.

role model (iron man dream #10)

I'm in a deserted restaurant with my brother.

we're standing in the dining area
        surrounded by empty tables + chairs
we're both grown men
we're talking.

in other dreams
        he's been a young boy
        or an angry accusing adult
but in this dream
        he's different
        more accepting of who I am.

the feeling between us is open + caring
        yet tentative
I can see that
        although he doesn't always understand me very well
        he cares about me + wants to support me somehow.

I say to him
        I guess iron man's not a very good
                role model for me, is he?

without judgement or criticism he replies
        no, I don't think he is.

athena (iron man dream #11)

I'm at my high school reunion
we're all dressed as super heroes
it's like a costume party.

I'm wearing my iron man outfit
I know it's just a costume
I'm wearing it because it's fun
         not because I need it.

there's a massive wall of mortar and stone nearby
it's obviously quite old
the edges and the corners are chipped
the surface is pitted and weathered
large cracks run deep into the center
it looks like part of some ancient fortress.

some of my old buddies from junior high
         have climbed up the front of the wall
they're hanging by their arms from heavy wooden posts
         that protrude from the stone facade
they seem happy there.

I move to the wall and start fooling around
         pulling at one corner until it begins to come loose
the wall starts to shift and wobble
my friends on the posts glare at me in disapproval
         as they swing back and forth with the wall
I've disturbed them.

suddenly a young woman appears
strong dark and purposeful
she's not one of us.

she too wears a costume
         but it's clear that her power is real
         not imagined

she's a warrior goddess
        dressed for battle in light armor
she's not fooling around.

without hesitation
        she goes to the wall and finishes the job I could
        only begin in my iron man disguise
she tears the crumbling facade to the ground and reveals
        what lies beyond.

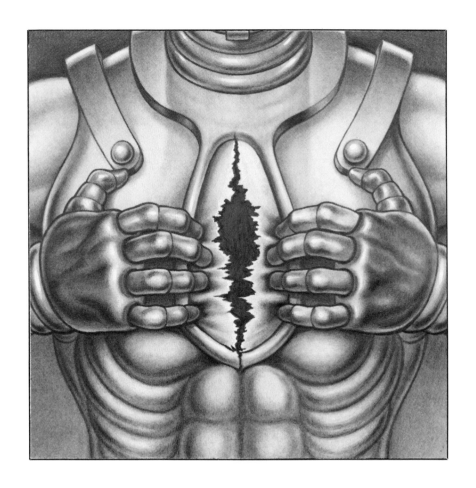

part five

———————— ■ ————————

shadowland

fear zone

howling dog in thunderstorm
        sunday morning
        2 am.

wake from family nightmare screaming
        gray light dawn
        single thunder
howling dog again.

alone again

fragile back   fragile knees
armor legs   armor heart
frightened groin   buzzard sun
hunting animal comfort
sick fly   bitter god
family fear   party heartbreak
hunting sex   repress mom vomit
sorry   miss you mom.

letdown treadmill   fractured soul
ghosts of twisted boyhood
killer foxes   sex salvation
hot   savage   criminal
always hole   never happy
tired back   injured knees
miss you dad   fix me dad
birthday   disappointed.

fragile sex fix burned me out
disappointed groin heart
mom needs me   dad dogs me
family funeral   grampa gone
burly iron man heartbreak deathtrap
miss you   love you   fix it for me grampa.

lunchbox deathtrap   software hardass
science fair salvation
frightened giants vomit onions   tired liver heat
bowel rage   funeral law   bitter family criminal
family needs me now and now and now . . .

noble catholic iron man injured
bowel hell   alone again
needs me needs me needs me burned out god
buzzards scream   foxes vomit   dogs rage
help me dad   love me dad
do it for me now!

lunatic son

go home + kill your father!
the guy's a dead dog heart attack!
he's a wind-jamming dancing bear with his foot in a trap!
kill him already! put him out of your misery!
quit bitchin' to your buddies + do it!
climb out of your murky hole + bludgeon the old fucker
        with the shovel he gave you!

blocked? jammed up? stuck?
kill dear old dad again!
smash his heavy metal belly like a burned-out bulb!
do your duty! find some heat!
smite the old soldier + feel the buzz!
turn up the radio!
dance like a stoned zombie!
dance like a straight arrow!
go home + kill your father!

face the hairy bastard!
distract him at the traffic light + then
        stomp his whiskered ass
        with your noisy young muscles!
shout out loud
        he's gone at last!
come out of your daze, you pathetic sleepwalker!
get a life! do yourself a big favor!
go home + kill your father + get it over with!

fever wheels

edgy empty heart
      spiteful child inside
rotting broken wings
      jealous chest rhythm
judge/decide/accuse.

mighty love trap triggers steel claws
pig-man + dog-woman fight for rotting fruit
itchy love toys fall from mattress
wheels spin off center into false machine.

hateful birds accuse me
elvis clones horse around
cool cats flock together
fever wheels turn . . .

I hate my friends today
it's not their fault but I hate them anyway because
      they can't help
      they can't do enough
      they can't fix it
      they can't fix me
they can't make it all right again.

broken concentration
standing in the hallway + shouting at god
      what do you want from me anyway
over + over + over
so sick of expecting too much.

love lies down with hate
I am their pretty pink child
      innocent + vengeful
      needy + ruthless
just gimme a chance
I will strike you down.

moral outrage puts me in the driver's seat
misplaced passion puts me on your back
without enemies I don't exist
without righteous anger I am undefined.

can't stand the company of others now
loneliness/isolation/alienation
        plunge me deeper into shadow
I'd rather be with those I despise than those I love
I'd rather poison myself than be poisoned by another.

can't stop   can't go forward
        trapped inside an empty tank
visions of crashing through the guardrails interfere
        with carefully planned progress
that's one way to break out I guess
god I thought I was through all that teenage stuff.

I thought I thought I thought
desperate to draw conclusions
        make pronouncements
        run scenarios
        formulate escape plans
that old dodge doesn't cut it anymore
this isn't something to figure out or get away from
no quick fix this time.

lost angry birds fly into my ears
tired nervous lungs stop dead in my chest
itchy trigger fingers rake through rotting red leaves
fever wheels turn . . .

I am in pain.

senseless

I'm trying to beat the truth out of myself
        beating myself senseless
visualizing world peace
        while I drive like a maniac.

x-ray barbeque

I rip my chest open I find
  blood maggots bricks dirt
  manure garbage two-by-four's
  nails rusty nails a claw hammer
  a bombed-out city a backed-up toilet
  a keg of fishhooks.

I rip my chest open I find
  snakes frogs lizards a black swamp
  nervous wolves flames heat prisoners
  a rack a wheel a dungeon
  rats ants cinder blocks fish heads.

I rip my chest open I find
  an animal on the highway
  flies swarming around restless corpses
  a bloated steaming raccoon carcass
  rotting raw meat broken bones torn flesh
  a hunting license a gun rack
  deer intestines in the snow
  severed pheasant heads + feet on newspaper
  empty shotgun shells.

I rip my chest open I find
  a slaughterhouse a press a torture chamber
  winged demons on ice
  evil farm animals up to no good
  an earthworm spilling its guts on a hook
  a neglected graveyard stones kicked over.

I rip my chest open I find
  shattered glass baseball bats a blacksmith anvil
  angry horses a rabid goat
  a frightened monkey in a space capsule
  a pressure cooker an incubator
  a shovel a knife a deep dark hole
and daylight.

harpies

I'm with my dad
we're in a house that's under construction
the wooden partition frames are up
        but there are no walls.

I confront him about
        the things he does
        the way he treats me
not from a place of anger hate + frustration
but from a place of real love for both of us.

he's hostile + tries to act threatening
        but I step closer to him
        closing the space between us until
        I'm right in his face
he backs away.

this happens several times.

I know that he can't hurt me now
I keep moving forward
        toward him
        asking questions
my protection comes from love
        rather than from anger.

eventually
        he begins to respond to my questions
        though in a halting defensive way
he seems tired old scared weak small.

a woman (his sister?) enters the room and interrupts us
she starts cutting him down for things he's done
I don't like her
she's a real petty bitch with a big ax to grind.

I'm upset with her for interfering
        just when my dad was starting to open up a little
I want to tell her to get lost.

another accusing woman joins her at this point
I feel outnumbered.

red meat head games

disappointed + angry today
           because I have to
    find some work
    soon
money-making work
I hate this.

here's what I value most:

      honesty   integrity   clarity
      independence   passion   freedom
      simplicity   awareness   nature.

here's what I see at work:

      lying greedy plastic noisy apathetic wasteful groupthink
      cowardly cynical carrot + stick
      sterile confusing corner-cutting crisis mode
      manipulation denial vampires
      drunken sugar overtime cocaine red meat head games
      upscale unconscious IRA adrenaline rush.

I guess I'm not a very good corporate soldier.

    I'm tired of sitting behind
someone else's desk
    doing
someone else's work
    living
someone else's life
    waiting for things to get better/worse.

always working faster + harder
    (we need it yesterday hahaha . . .)

to provide more
         technology
to make our lives faster + harder
         more confusing
                  more complicated
                           more dangerous
                           less conscious
                  less meaningful
         less personal
less human.

let's slow this thing down folks
         I don't know about you but
my techno wet dream's over.

disconnected

the space walk is over
someone has cut the umbilical cord
the astronaut is disconnected from the spacecraft
he flaps + kicks but drifts away
he shouts + cries but isn't heard
soon he will run out of air
maybe he'll bump into another spacecraft first
the others go on about their business.

part six

---- ■ ----

the unclaimed soul

water long gone

in a dry creek bed filled with fallen brown leaves
I sit among the stones
  back tight as a snare drum skin
  restless as winter wind through lifeless branches
staring at lines
  left by water long gone.

elephant dream

I have in my care three elephants
        two males   one female
they are very sick
        from too much time in the heat of the sun
they've come to a place of shade and safety now
        but they're dying
the female is the sickest.

they have large ragged holes in their skins
        burned into them by an unforgiving sun
weak and withered
dried and dying
drained of power
        they wait and they suffer.

I've noticed them only recently
I know that without my help
        their time is short.

I haven't been trained to care for these holy creatures
        so I ask others for help
one well-intentioned man
        young bureaucrat in uniform
        suggests a cage for shade and safety
they're dying!
        I remind him
but they'll be very safe
        he says.

others are not interested at all
some make jokes
this is urgent! who will help me?

these animals need water
        lots of it

more than I can ever provide
     with the old buckets once used by
     my father   my uncles   my grandfathers
elephants have other needs too
     but water is basic and must come first.

I'm desperate   time is short
I walk up a slow hill on a back country road
     (I've walked this road in younger days)
looking for someone to help me save these sacred beasts.

charley horse

leg hurting tonight reminds me of how my dad + I used to
        run across each other in the dark
        when I was little + my leg would hurt.

he had a lot of leg cramps at night
he called that *a goddam charley horse*
I used to wake up with intense pain in my leg
        the leg I broke
        trying to catch up with him
when I was first learning to walk.

sometimes we'd both wake up at the same time
        on the same night
I liked this because I got to spend some quiet time
        alone with him.

I never wanted to go back to bed on those nights
we'd sit in the living room or the kitchen
        in the dark or with a dim light on
he seemed more open in those moments
I didn't feel like he hated me then
maybe it was because he was sleepy
        or in pain.

those were special occasions for me
        nothing to accomplish or be judged on
we each had our own pain
        similar but not the same
he was empathetic
I felt connected to him.

in those brief moments
I always felt that I was just like him
        just like I always wanted to be.

plastic bones

whenever we speak
      you toss me quick platitudes
plastic bones
      to a hungry dog.

plow my heart

sick of the fleshy freak show
down on the bad boy side show
money doesn't bring closeness
dead soldiers overload the heartbreak system.

disappointed farmers plow my heart
drive their tractors through my chest
plant corn in the ventricles
            tomatoes in the aorta
wash the moss from the abandoned valves
            + wait for next year's harvest.

sometimes they flood the chambers with smoke
            so it doesn't get too cold in there
sometimes deer come + eat the corn
sometimes the farmers go fishing
            instead of tending the field
but the fish are angry
            the earthworms are violent
            the bridge is painful
            the farmers return home filled with regret.

how have I come to such a place
drugs + fake lightning do not drain the well of shame
shame does not feed the corn
shame feeds the darkness
shame is food for the goners.

I should be crying now but I'm not
I should be grieving now but I'm not
I'm the quiet good boy
            jumping for the dust mop
            organized + clean
I'm the big mouth bad boy
            lobbing sex grenades at the silky slinky thighs
            deep in the mushrooms on a low budget

waiting for the end of the day
faithful to my creed . . .

> *I will not fall down again*
> *I will not fall down.*

I will not fall
I will not fail
I will not feel.

hoofbeats

horses
running horses
sad running horses
      sad horses
      saw horses
I saw horses
I saw sad running horses
running horses
sad.

close to it

my grandfather
        my father's father
                has just died.

the whole family is grieving his death
the wake is being held at
        some sort of athletic field
my dad sits alone up in the bleachers
        away from the others
I go up there to talk with him.

I can barely keep from crying as I sit beside him
I'm sad to have lost my grandfather
        but most of my tears are for my dad
I can see that he's suffering
        but he can't express his sadness
        although he is so close to it
                so very close to it
as I am close to mine.

bridge to gate

I'm visiting my grandmother.

she shows me a narrow earthen bridge
       that crosses the pond beside her house
she tells me
       we built this bridge for you
she encourages me to use it.

I study the bridge
I notice that here + there
       the surface of the bridge is covered
       by a thin layer of water
just enough to get my feet wet.

then I see a gate
       at the far end of the bridge
       on the other side of the pond
the gate is closed.

at the sight of the closed gate
       I want to give up
but in my heart I know
       that if I cross the water
       the gate will open.

touch the water

water's edge
      white ducks + black swans
feathers   leaves
      plastic spoon
      plants   algae   moss
a grackle
sawed-off bushes
rocks + mud.

so much water
      cold dark + clear
I sit on the edge
      no reflection
      mesmerized + hurting
afraid to touch the water
afraid to go in.

pearls

I wait for tears to come gently
        like soft spring rain
tears that will fall like diamonds
        from the sky
wise little pearls
        harvested at great expense
she doesn't want me anymore.

grief

grief is a chapter in a book
grief is the playmate of the year
grief is the tenth planet of the solar system
grief is a painting in a cave
grief is a controlled substance
grief is a cure for cancer
grief is a cure for the common cold
grief is a walk on the moon.

grief is a movie that doesn't start on time
grief is the pythagorean theorem
grief is a science fair project
grief is a frog in formaldehyde
grief is my favorite martian.

grief is a dog being chased by a car
grief is a tray of ice cubes in the freezer
grief is an empty cardboard box
grief is dry heaves on sunday night
grief is a naked mannequin
grief is a national geographic special.

grief is a slide rule
grief is a lawn mower engine
grief is a welding rod
grief is a monday morning
grief is a friday night.

grief is a cooking class
grief is a noisy dog
grief is a topless bar
grief is a chest x-ray
grief is a shot fired through a ghost
grief is an animal at the zoo
grief is a caved-in coal mine.

decision time again

I'm in a flat area
there are
>no trees
>no people
>no buildings
the grass is very short.

there are several intersecting dirt roads
it's like
>I'm in the midwest
>I'm in the middle
>I'm in the middle of somewhere
it's an open empty place
>nowhere to hide.

I have to keep making decisions about
>which way to go
I've been doing this for a while now + still
>somehow I'm
>>a little frustrated
>>a little confused.

I'm on a trip but I have no clear idea of
>where I'm going or
>how long it will take.

part seven

hints of daylight

starfall

stars in my eyes
       stars on my plate
              stars land on rooftops
                     stars fall on cars.

stars hit the pavement
       stars hit the beach
              stars underwater
                     stars out of reach.

difficult

so sad today
why is it so difficult for me to have what I want
      why does it take so long.

I don't wanna make more weapons
      for the overstocked arsenal
I don't wanna flood the market
      with more useless escapist junk
I don't wanna pollute our homes + hearts + minds
I don't wanna tell someone else what to do
I don't wanna acquire more things
I don't wanna make more money.

I want to be
      the turtle on the log
      the rock in the water
      the breeze thru the branches
      the napping duck
      the flapping wings
      the overcast sky
      the woodpecker in the tree
      the cat clawing at the stump
      the lazy grass
      the barking squirrel.

why is this so much to ask.

why is this so difficult.

brown-eyed boy

I'm trying to make friends with a little brown-eyed boy
he doesn't trust me.

I've made and broken many promises to him in the past
      and he's angry with me
he's frustrated because I often forget he's there
      or ignore him
      or pretend he doesn't matter
      or make fun of him
      or leave him with others
         who don't value him for who he is
he's afraid of me.

his feelings are strong
he knows what he wants
I don't trust him.

he's curious   alert   he understands things quickly
he knows what he wants
I'm afraid of him.

we share a common sadness that neither shows the other
we haven't treated each other well over the years
we didn't know how
sometimes we come together now
      with a cat in our lap or a bat in our hands.

the other day I saw he needed help
I offered myself to him
      but he turned his back to the world and said
no! I want daddy to help me with that.

wounded man detection device (from john lee)

he has a dysfunctional or non-existent relationship
    with his father
he is extremely close to his mother + is seen by her
    as savior or saint
he is often described as intense
he thrives on drama.

he is extremely close to his mother + is seen by her
    as savior or saint
he is often described as dark melancholy or depressed
he thrives on drama
he complains about not having enough energy.

he is often described as dark melancholy or depressed
he has a history of not committing to jobs places
    people + projects
he complains about not having enough energy
he has a rigid body structure.

he has a history of not committing to jobs places
    people + projects
he is a workaholic or can't find a job worthy of his
    time or talents
he has a rigid body structure
he is potentially creative + yet unable to produce.

he is a workaholic or can't find a job worthy of his
    time or talents
he has a history of drug or alcohol abuse
he is potentially creative + yet unable to produce
he thinks he is in touch with his feelings.

he has a history of drug or alcohol abuse
he always needs to be in control of himself others
    + situations
he thinks he is in touch with his feelings
he is seldom spontaneous.

he always needs to be in control of himself others
        + situations
he is overly analytical
he is seldom spontaneous
he is highly critical.

he is overly analytical
he is constantly striving towards perfection
he is highly critical
he is unable to express anger appropriately.

he is constantly striving towards perfection
he is spiritual to an extreme degree
he is unable to express anger appropriately
he can't say no except to the woman he loves.

he is spiritual to an extreme degree
he is often described as intense
he can't say no except to the woman he loves
he has a dysfunctional or non-existent relationship
        with his father.

body memory

my elbow remembers
     riding my rocking horse off the front porch
my skin remembers
     slap of the flyswatter metal wire handle
my tongue remembers
     bar of soap shoved in my mouth
my hand remembers
     spilled milk on the first day of first grade
my stomach remembers
     crying in front of everyone 'cause I lost the fight
my knee remembers
     wait for me daddy before I fell + broke my leg
my feet remember
     please teach ricky how to skip
     pinned to my kindergarten shirt
my chin remembers
     falling out of bed into a
     daddy's mad again hot sunday night
my nose remembers
     can't breathe comic books in ragweed darkness
my fingers remember
     building model rockets in a cool summer basement
my neck remembers
     father's hands closing tight around my throat
my ears remember
     mother screaming *stop it dick stop it.*

time passes but nothing is lost
I can't fool myself
my body remembers everything.

acceptance

for me
acceptance isn't
      that's in the past
      did the best they could
      nothing I can do about it
      everything's great now
      don't care anyway
      I give up.

for me
acceptance is
      I don't like it
      I'm not ready yet
      I'm frustrated today
      I want my dad
      I'm still hurting
      I'm still pissed
and it's ok for me to be like this.

learning to breathe

I'm learning to breathe again
    but it's painful.

when I breathe I feel
    the pressure of my sorrow
    the weight of 10,000 uncried tears.

when I breathe I feel
    the power of my shame
    a jagged chunk of black ice lodged
        deep in my throat.

when I breathe I feel
    the animal life
        animal fear + animal sadness
        animal panic + animal loss.

when I breathe I feel
    the screws in my chest beginning to loosen
    + the life I've known for so long
        coming to an end.

release

the injured tree chops away at its own roots
      every limb an ax
it claws and tears at the life-giving earth
      demands to be moved and stubbornly struggles
      to pull itself out of the ground.

reaching skyward
it pulls down the clouds
      surrounding itself in their darkness
      then cursing the absence of light.

it punches at the wind and the rain
      a mighty fist that never connects
it rages at the sun and the moon for being so far away.

years pass but
      the earth does not yield
      the wind and rain keep coming
      the sun and moon are what they are
the tree begins to see . . .

I didn't choose these wounds
      but they're mine
I didn't choose this place
      but here I am.

I lay down my axes
      and let go the clouds
I dance with the wind
      and sing with the rain
I laugh with the sun
      and cry with the moon.

I live and give thanks for joy and pain
      another day.

easter

in this dream
I'm looking at an old family photo
        25-year-old black + white
mother father brother + me
        the classic easter pose in the yard
                outside grandpa + grandma's house
my focus is on my dad
he's so young
        younger than I am now
and he looks so scared!

I feel compassion + tenderness for this
        frightened young man who took on too much
                a family he was ill-prepared to handle.

I know some of his fear
I feel it myself in my own life every day
        the fear of being a bad father
        the fear of being a father too soon
        the fear of losing my life + my dreams to
                the demands of a wife + a child
he has good reason to be afraid
he looks lonely
no one's taught him how to do this
nobody's backing him up.

I feel his loneliness + his fear for the first time
        not in my head but in my heart + my gut
I'm surprised to feel such thorough compassion for him
        as he was at that time
I'm so used to hating the man I knew as my father
        angry insensitive frightening hateful cruel
I don't feel comfortable identifying with
        this man I've cast as my personal demon.

this dream frightens me because I'm afraid I'm like him
        but it also encourages me

it tells me that
> maybe I'm beginning to see him as a person
> > instead of a demon
> maybe I'm beginning to let go of him at last.

autonomy

standing
      front yard
            grampagramma's farmhouse.

father sun + mother moon
      set behind me
           twilight west
while morning sun
      rises before me
           daybreak east.

it's my life now.

x-it wound

I did what the man suggested
I went deep into the wound
I hitched a ride on the pain express
        through the tunnels in my chest
        into that hairy heart of darkness
                everyone's always yapping about
        and I lived to tell about it.

it's been months and now I'm tired
        I need a break
        I need to do nothing
        I need to go back outside
I need to leave this place for a while
before all the blackness swallows me up.

my reflection's getting fuzzy
I feel my blood starting to ooze through my pores
dizzy spells
insomnia
blurred vision
I almost fell in the shower today
        I need food + rest
        I need to dance + sing
                to let the tears come.

it's time to stop talking + start walking.

I don't have to do this all at once
        there's plenty of time
I'll be back.

listen . . .

there's a blue steel train inside me
rolling down the tracks in the starlight
past the dark slumbering houses.

there's a hungry child inside me
crying to be fed
dying to be held
starving to be loved.

there's a lonely wolf inside me
standing on an empty hill in the moonlight
howling for his long lost mate.

there's a civil war inside me
father against son
son against father
blood on the family tree.

there's a brand-new day inside me
a fresh breeze blowing
a warm sun rising
and a sleeping bird about to awake.

Iron Man Family Outing is printed in a limited edition of 2000 copies the first 400 of which are signed and numbered.